Original title:
The Apple Blossom

Copyright © 2025 Creative Arts Management OÜ
All rights reserved.

Author: Matthew Whitaker
ISBN HARDBACK: 978-1-80586-400-4
ISBN PAPERBACK: 978-1-80586-872-9

Delicate Echoes of Spring

In a garden where pixies play,
Petals giggle in bright array.
Bees wear hats, sipping some tea,
While flowers dance with utmost glee.

Bunnies bounce with silly cheer,
Wearing sunglasses, oh so near.
They hop in circles, round and round,
Chasing their tails without a sound.

A squirrel struts in search of snacks,
Jumps on a branch, then does a backtrack.
With every leap, a chuckle's sound,
As nature's comedy knows no bounds.

So come and join this fragrant jest,
Where blooms and blooms take on a quest.
In this lighthearted, sunny space,
Springtime gives the world a happy face.

The Fruit of Tender Moments

In the orchard, giggles rise,
Bumbling bees with silly ties.
A squirrel hops, it trips and slides,
Chasing dreams, where fun resides.

Bright green leaves wave cheerfully,
Frogs croak tunes, a symphony.
Dancing foxes join the show,
With their paws, they steal the glow.

Warm sun beams, a gentle tease,
Fruit of laughter stirs the breeze.
It's a feast of playful cheer,
Nature's joy is always near.

Round and plump, a merry sight,
Juicy bites, what pure delight!
In this park of jolly sounds,
Tender moments know no bounds.

Nature's Blush

In the garden, colors fight,
Flowers blush, oh what a sight!
Bumblebees in fancy hats,
Buzzing round like acrobats.

Laughter echoes through the air,
Sunlight dances everywhere.
Wiggly worms do silly flips,
Waving flags with leafy tips.

Petals whisper, secrets shared,
Windswept dramas, none are scared.
Butterflies in polka dots,
Twirl and spin in photo spots.

Nature's smile can't be contained,
With each giggle, all's regained.
Spin and twirl, let's make amends,
In this swirl, we're all great friends.

Vitality in Every Bloom

Tiny sprouts in playful rows,
Chasing sunlight, watch them grow!
With each bloom, a story starts,
Nature's canvas, painted hearts.

Bouncing bunnies with big dreams,
Hop around and share their schemes.
Radishes in wigs of green,
Laughing at the silly scene.

Chirping birds in clever hats,
Tweet their jokes like acrobat!
Smiling clouds peek down to play,
Joining in on this fine day.

Each petal offers something sweet,
Joyful notes in every beat.
A garden full of vibrant shouts,
Blooming life, and fun throughout.

Mornings Dressed in Pink

Awake at dawn, the sun is shy,
With pink pajamas in the sky.
Frogs wear crowns, they serenade,
Each little splash, a grand parade.

Cherries giggle on the trees,
Dancing lightly in the breeze.
Birds in tuxedos fly about,
Offering jokes with playful shout.

Blushing flowers, all aglow,
Winking petals, stealing shows.
Nature craves a morning laugh,
Snickers bounce like joyful half.

So grab your snacks, let smiles bloom,
In this garden, there's no gloom.
With morning's cheer, we make a pact,
To find the fun and joy intact.

Blossoms Embrace the Sun

In the garden, blooms do sway,
Chasing light throughout the day.
Bees wear tiny sunglasses bright,
Buzzworthy vibes, what a sight!

Petals giggle in the breeze,
A dance party among the trees.
With every twist and silly twirl,
Nature's fun, a joyful whirl!

When Springtime Wakes the Land

Awake, asleep, the flowers tease,
With whispers carried on the breeze.
They shout, 'Hey, it's time to play!'
As worms in hats worm their way!

Chirping birds join in the chat,
While bunnies hop in silly hats.
The sun's a jester, shining bright,
Springtime's here, it's pure delight!

Tapestry of Buds Unfurled

A tapestry of colors blooms,
Each blossom breaks out from their rooms.
With petals painted bright and bold,
They laugh at winter, feeling cold!

The tulips wear polka dots so neat,
While daisies dance with dainty feet.
In this garden, fun's the rule,
Who knew flowers were so cool?

Petals Fall Like Gentle Rain

Petals drop, a floral shower,
Turning sidewalks into a bower.
Children catch them, giggle and fumble,
While squirrels conspire and tumble!

The air is filled with sweet perfume,
As blooms take over every room.
With flowers laughing all around,
Spring's giggles are the best sound!

Elysian Fields of Blossom Dreams

In a garden where giggles go,
Chasing petals that dance to and fro.
Bumblebees buzzing with boisterous glee,
Hiding sweet secrets for you and me.

Snails wear hats, so dapper and bright,
They race through the greens with all of their might.
The daisies roll over, they can't help but cheer,
As the tulips trade jokes, it's the best time of year!

Fragile Moments Awash in Light

A ladybug drops in for tea,
Sipping nectar while hanging from a tree.
Sunshine tickles the leaves with delight,
Making shadows dance in a whimsical flight.

Butterflies chatter with colorful decks,
Trading bad puns and gentle head pecks.
It's a roguish realm, where laughter's the crown,
In the petals' embrace, no need for a frown.

Serenity Found in Nature's Embrace.

Worms wear the wildest of wigs,
Grinning as they wiggle like jigs.
With every squirm, they evoke a loud laugh,
Creating a symphony with just their half!

Birds on their branches gossip and chirp,
Trading sweet jokes with a cheeky little burp.
Dandelions snicker, they float in the breeze,
Cheering for friends, as the world seeks to tease.

Whispers of Spring's Awakening

Giggling grass finds its tickling toes,
While flowers come up for a cheerful nose.
Tickled by breezes that make them sway,
They giggle and shimmer in a playful ballet.

Crickets in tuxedos dance under the moon,
Hopping in rhythm, they burst into tune.
Laughter erupts from the earth's tender skin,
In the funniest bloom, let the fun begin!

A Cornucopia of Color

In spring they pop up, bright and bold,
Their petals giggle, secrets unfold.
One's a clown with a polka dot dress,
While another tries to impress, no less.

The bees play tag as they buzz around,
Dancing in circles, it's joy they've found.
Each bud's a contestant in nature's fair show,
With laughter and colors, they steal the show.

Blooming Through the Seasons

From winter's snooze to summer's cheer,
They sprout with glee, with no trace of fear.
In rain or shine, they toss their heads,
Singing sweet tunes as they dress their beds.

Autumn and winter can't dampen their fun,
Making snowballs with petals just for a run.
They play peek-a-boo with the frosty air,
Wearing coats of white, no time for despair.

Celestial Delights

Stars of the garden, shining so bright,
In a cosmic ballet, taking flight.
They twinkle in colors, a riot of cheer,
Winking at passersby, drawing them near.

With a giggle and twist, they flirt with the breeze,
Wrapping confetti in sunlight with ease.
Space cadets just floating, having a blast,
Reminding us joy is never too fast.

The Dance of Future Fruits

Tiny green globes are shaking their hips,
Plotting charades with sneaky little flips.
They dream of being pies, or perhaps a tart,
With sweeter plans, they're off to a start.

With each sway and jiggle, they charm the sun,
Preparing for the banquet, oh what fun!
They know when they're ripe, it's time for a feast,
Baking up laughter, we'll savor the least!

A Canvas of Petals

In the orchard, colors clash,
Bees with hats, they start to mash.
Petals dance, a wild ballet,
Squirrels giggle, come what may.

Branches wobble, a mischief spree,
Laughing birds join in with glee.
A painter with a goofy brush,
Colors splash, an artistic hush.

Fruits whisper secrets low and near,
While butterflies toast with a cheer.
Nature's quirk, a vibrant show,
Joyful chaos, watch it grow.

With every wind, a chuckle blown,
In this garden, laughter's grown.
Petals plop, a funny sight,
Life's a jest, pure delight.

Echoes of Sweetness

In the air, a sugary tease,
Ants are dancing, doing the squeeze.
Flavors mingle, a sweet parade,
Buzzing friends in a clumsy charade.

Cherries giggle, ripe and round,
Roll off branches, hit the ground.
A bumblebee, wearing a tie,
Stumbles over, oh my, oh my!

Whispers of sugar fill the breeze,
Nature chuckles, aims to please.
Clouds burst laughter, drops of gold,
Stories sweet, forever told.

Giggles burst in every turn,
As blossoms wave and brightly burn.
Underneath the laughing sky,
A world of sweetness, oh me, oh my!

Entwined with the Breeze

A jaunty breeze plays peek-a-boo,
Twirling blossoms, oh what a view!
Critters join in, a funny dance,
Each petal pirouettes in a trance.

Grass tickles toes of passing feet,
Every step brings groovy beat.
Clouds chuckle, puffing like a cake,
Nature's whimsy, make no mistake.

A daisy dons a tiny hat,
Winks at the worm, how about that?
Sun shines bright, a playful jest,
In this party, we are blessed.

With laughter swirling through the land,
Joyful chaos, hand in hand.
Breeze tickles secrets in the air,
Life's a joke, everywhere!

Painting Dreams in Bloom

A canvas spread where colors blend,
Bees paint buzzes, a joyful trend.
Petals giggle, splashing hues,
Nature's palette, silly views.

Little worms in a parade,
Belly flops in the sun, unafraid.
Twirling flowers, swaying like pros,
A riot of laughter as the breeze blows.

Echoes of joy in a vibrant heap,
Chasing shadows, never sleep.
Brush strokes of laughter fill the sky,
Watch as giggles flutter by.

A brush in sunshine, coast to coast,
Painting dreams, we laugh the most.
In every bloom, a story glows,
Life's a canvas, may it pose!

Beneath the Petal Canopy

In a garden full of chatter,
The bees hold a debate.
They buzz about the sweet taste,
Of fruit that's on their plate.

Petals dance like clowns above,
Waving to the sky.
A ladybug just winked at me,
As if to say, 'Oh my!'

The breeze joins in the giggles,
Tickling leaves with glee.
I laugh when branches bow so low,
As if they lost their key.

Underneath this flowery tent,
We tell our silliest tales.
The sunlight shines, the butterflies,
Turn whispers into wails.

Singing with the Wind

A squirrel serenades the trees,
With acorns in his stash.
The wind picks up his chirpy notes,
And makes them into trash.

The robins join in harmony,
While dancing on a plume.
They chirp and hop with glee around,
To chase away the gloom.

With every twist the branches make,
They jive without a care.
A gust of wind blows through the boughs,
Like laughter in the air.

And as I bounce along with them,
I hear a funny tune.
The blossoms giggle loud with me,
Beneath a leafy moon.

The Language of Flowers

In the garden of polite blooms,
The violets put on airs.
They gossip 'bout the lilacs' style,
And other flower flares.

Roses speak in whispers,
With thorns they toss around.
While daisies shout, 'We're number one!'
In their floral playground.

Tulips twirl in polka dots,
While sunflowers stand tall.
In this chatty patch of petals,
Humor cracks through them all.

Laughter blooms in every bud,
As colors clash and play.
With every joke they toss about,
They brighten up the day.

An Orchard's Lull

In the orchard, silence falls,
But apples giggle loud.
They tickle each other swiftly,
Behind a leafy shroud.

Cherries wear a rosy grin,
As they sway in delight.
They bounce around and play peek-a-boo,
Through branches out of sight.

Plums puff up with pride, you know,
For their royal purple hue.
While oranges are cracking jokes,
As citrus does, it's true!

As dusk arrives, the laughter fades,
But dreams are still in bloom.
In slumber, fruits exchange their gags,
Beneath the harvest moon.

Bloom and Bough in Harmony

In the garden where laughter flies,
Buds chuckle under sunny skies.
Leaves wiggle with a silly cheer,
Nature giggles as spring draws near.

A bumblebee bustles with a grin,
Dancing 'round, ready to spin.
The flowers wink, what a delight,
In this crazy, colorful sight.

A squirrel in boots tries to frolic,
Tripping over roots, oh so comedic!
The breeze whispers jokes, so spry,
While robins laugh and never shy.

Sunshine tickles branches high,
As butterflies flutter, oh me, oh my!
In this quirky patch of mirth,
Nature's humor brings sweet rebirth.

Pale Pink Dreams Ignite

A blossom smiles with rosy face,
While a kitten finds a sunny place.
Pale pink dreams dance with delight,
Chasing shadows in the light.

The petals pop, a party grows,
While ants do the cha-cha in rows.
Laughter echoes through the air,
As nature shows off, what a flair!

Buds tease the bees, whispering low,
"Check this out! It's quite the show!"
Grasshoppers leap with tricks to share,
While the daisies giggle without a care.

In this whimsy, we all partake,
With every wiggle, every shake.
A funny scene unfolds, just right,
As pale pink dreams ignite the night.

A Symphony of Fragile Hues

A symphony of colors unfolds,
As stories of spring are humorously told.
Each hue a giggle, each shape a jest,
Nature's comedy, simply the best!

Petals persuade the wind to dance,
While clouds float by in a silly trance.
Butterflies join in the playful tune,
As the sun plays peek-a-boo with the moon.

A daffodil dons a jaunty hat,
While daisies gossip, getting all fat.
The chorus of blooms in joyful sway,
Makes the garden a cabaret display.

With every rustle, a chuckle's born,
As the blossoms boast at the break of dawn.
In this hilarious botanical spree,
Every leaf laughs along with glee!

Nectar's Dance on Soft Stems

On soft stems, sweet nectar pours,
As critters burst through flowering doors.
A bumblebee sings a silly song,
While the ants tap dance all day long.

The flora flutter in comical ways,
As morning sun begins to blaze.
Beetles glide in tuxedos bright,
Making a ruckus from day to night.

Blossoms tease with fragrant sighs,
As ladybugs wink with tiny eyes.
In this frolic, joy's contagious,
Every petal's grin is outrageous!

A dance-off blooms with nature's flair,
While clouds float lazily, unaware.
In this garden, with laughter abound,
The nectar's dance is truly renowned.

Pink Veils Against the Sky

Pink veils flutter in the breeze,
Gathering gossip from the trees.
They dance and wiggle, oh so spry,
Whispering secrets, oh my, oh my!

Bees wear sunglasses, quite the sight,
Buzzing around with pure delight.
They mock the blooms with cheeky grins,
Claiming the nectar now belongs to them!

Flowers giggle as they bloom,
Causing mishaps across the room.
Hats fly off each surprised head,
Chasing petals as they spread.

With each sway, they start to tease,
Colorful pranks that aim to please.
Nature's jesters, bright and spry,
Winking at birds that flutter by.

Blossoms of Renewal

Fresh blooms pop like bubble wrap,
Springtime's here, let's take a nap.
Pink fluff covers the ground like snow,
More surprising than a squirrel in a bow!

Tulips wear sneakers, run in style,
Daffodils dance; oh, stay awhile!
They challenge each other to a race,
Pollen flying, what a wild place!

Buds are peeking, shy and bright,
"Look at us!" they shout with delight.
A playful breeze gives them a shove,
Whirling through gardens they truly love.

With laughter, the petals lose their cool,
Flirty flowers, oh, what a jewel!
Each bloom, a joke waiting to unfold,
Making springtime stories bold!

Orchard Serenade

In orchards bursting with color and grin,
The blossoms hum a tune to begin.
Bouncing bees bring the beat alive,
As playful petals jump and jive.

Birds join in, each one a star,
Singing loudly, near and far.
A harmonica just hitched a ride,
With a flower band, nothing to hide.

The squirrels, with flair, patter along,
Giggling as they join the song.
Chasing shadows, making a fuss,
A comical scene, no need to rush.

As twilight falls, the mood is light,
Blossoms whisper, "What a sight!"
With each laugh, nature's true cheer,
A funny chorus for all to hear!

Blossoms Awaken the Heart

Once upon a bud, sweet and shy,
A burst of laughter caught my eye.
Blossoms grinning, oh what a tease,
They tickle dreams like a gentle breeze.

With a wink, they sprout in piles,
Giggles echo through their aisles.
Fluttering petals, quite the show,
Who knew flowers had so much glow?

Joking trees sway their branches wide,
All the critters take great pride!
"Come dance with us!" they seem to shout,
While bouncing blooms flit here and about.

As sunsets color the fields anew,
Nature smiles with a lightened hue.
The world awakens with joy and art,
Thanks to the giggles that warm the heart.

Whispers of Spring's Petals

In the garden, laughter grows,
Funny faces, where no one knows.
Bumblebees buzz with silly glee,
Dancing round, oh let them be!

Petals giggle, tickled by air,
Winking at folks with nary a care.
Squirrels wearing hats made of green,
A sight so odd, it's truly seen!

Children leap with joyous shouts,
Chasing shadows, running about.
Sprinkling cheer like flower seeds,
Funny moments sprout from needs!

Nature grins in colors bright,
Jokes unfold in morning light.
A parade of blooms, what a scene,
Springtime's jesters, pure and keen!

Sweet Fragrance in the Breeze

The sun's up high, the day is new,
Sniff the air, oh, what a hue!
A fruity scent wafts all around,
What's that smell? It's quite profound!

A rabbit hops in floral shoes,
Sharing secrets with the snooze.
With flowers that tickle noses,
A garden party no one supposes!

Breezes tickle with a wink,
Catch that scent, or you might sink!
Into a daydream made of fun,
With aromas kissed by the sun!

Pollen dances, insects hum,
In the orchard, giggles come.
A fragrance quite absurdly sweet,
Making all of spring a treat!

Beneath the Glistening Tree

In the shade where giggles lay,
Fruit hangs like jokes on display.
A plump one rolls, the kids all squeal,
A puddle of laughter, a silly meal!

Beneath the branches, shadows play,
Wiggling worms in quite the ballet.
Who knew nature had such flair?
With every squirm, it's sure to share!

Sunshine dapples with a tease,
Trees wear crowns, it's such a breeze.
Branches sway like they tell jokes,
And every chuckle, the laughter pokes!

A picnic blanket, a food galore,
But ants steal snacks—oh, what a chore!
Nature's humor, quite the spree,
Underneath this silly tree!

Secrets of Orchard's Heart

In the orchard, whispers flow,
With secrets that the blossoms know.
An old crow caws with gentle sass,
Telling tales of flowers' class!

Rabbits gossip 'round the roots,
While squirrels wear their fancy boots.
The pears so ripe do giggle and sway,
As fruit flies dance through a sunny ballet!

Each bloom hides a chuckle bright,
With petals grinning in sheer delight.
Nature plays the jester's part,
In this lively, funny heart!

As laughter bursts, there's no end,
To the funny ways that blossoms blend.
Secrets bursting with every beat,
In the orchard, life's a treat!

Shadows Dance with Light

In the garden, shadows twirl,
Chasing light like a silly pearl.
Leaves are giggling in the breeze,
While a worm sings, "Oh, look at me!"

Flowers prance in bright display,
Petal hats on heads, they sway.
Buzzing bees join in the show,
Dancing round like they don't know.

A caterpillar trips and falls,
He bumps his head, the laughter calls.
Ladybugs wear spots with pride,
While grasshoppers jump far and wide.

Amidst the humor and delight,
Nature's charm feels just so right.
As long as sunshine paints the day,
We'll laugh and frolic all the way!

Blossoms on the Wind

Petals whirl like dancers bold,
Spinning tales of springtime gold.
A tiny bird just lost its socks,
Flapping wildly, "What a shock!"

Breezes toss the blooms about,
A daisy shouts, "Come, let's all shout!"
Chasing clouds that look like sheep,
They giggle softly, watch them leap.

A butterfly with oversized shades,
Sips sweet nectar and parades.
While ants in line pass by with flair,
Waving their antennas in the air.

Every flower wears a grin,
Nature's jesters tucked within.
So let the colors paint the scene,
As joy unfolds in vivid green!

Whispered Promises of Warmth

A whisper here, a giggle there,
Sunshine teasing with extra flair.
The trees exchange their silly jokes,
While sneaky squirrels chuckle and poke.

A raindrop lands on a thirsty leaf,
"Is that a shower or just a brief?"
Crickets chirp with comic tones,
As daisies nod on leafy thrones.

With clouds that puff like cotton candy,
The bumblebee's dance is rather dandy.
While vines entwine, they play a game,
"Who can wiggle!" they cheer, untame.

So bright, the day with laughter's tune,
Nature sings beneath the moon.
In every leaf and every sprout,
A promise of fun, without a doubt!

In the Embrace of Change

Windy whispers, strange and sweet,
Leaves twist up while we stomp our feet.
A pumpkin smiles, quite out of place,
As if it's joined a lively race.

Breezes carry stories old,
Of ants that march in paths of gold.
A fallen branch gets dressed with cheer,
"I think I'll be a slide this year!"

Sowing seeds of mischievous glee,
Nature coaxes you and me.
While branches wave in playful jest,
It's all a game; it's all a fest!

From blossoms bright to autumn's hue,
The seasons change, yet laugh anew.
So let us dance in shifts and sways,
In this embrace of funny ways!

Navigating Through Bloom

In a garden full of cheer,
A bee trips on a flower's ear.
With pollen all around,
He buzzes, tumbles, hits the ground.

The petals giggle, 'What a sight!'
The buzzing dance, a comical flight.
A caterpillar nods with glee,
'Next time, wear a map, not just a spree!'

Amidst the scents, a breeze does tease,
A squirrel joins, balancing with ease.
He slips, he slides, but no harm done,
Lands on a patch of grass, just for fun.

Symphony of Nature's Rhythm

The frogs croak in a rhythm so grand,
A squirrel conducts with a tiny hand.
The worms wiggle in tune with the rain,
While the daisies clap on the windowpane.

A robin takes the lead for a song,
Strutting like he really belongs.
A chorus of bees join in for a buzz,
While ants march along, because, why not, cause?

The leaves sway, trying to dance,
While a butterfly flaunts its colorful prance.
But the wind whips and tangles a vine,
As the flowers all huddle and say, 'Not so fine!'

Flourish and Flourish

Bright petals stretching to the sun,
Family flowers having so much fun.
A sunflower claims, 'I'm the tallest here,'
While the tulips giggle, whispering, 'Oh dear!'

The daisies compete for the prettiest pose,
With a wink and a smile, they strike a rose.
All of a sudden, a woodpecker taps,
Reminding them all they need to relax!

'Flourish and flourish!' the daisies cheer loud,
'Be proud of your roots, we're a fabulous crowd!'
With laughter and mirth in the warm sun's glow,
Even the weeds smile, 'We all steal the show!'

Unveiling the Green

In the garden, surprises await,
Weeds pop up, oh, isn't that great?
A gnome chuckles, 'What a wild scene!'
As a nosey snail acts like a queen.

The grass tries its best to stand tall,
While flowers giggle, having a ball.
An earthworm wiggles, 'Look at me shine!'
'Glamorous mud, it's simply divine!'

With every new bud, the laughter unfolds,
While critters share stories that joyfully mold.
In this mischievous patch, life takes its spin,
Unveiling the green, let the fun begin!

Ephemeral Joys

In springtime's grin, the petals sway,
Bugs in top hats dance every day.
A bee does a jig, then slips on a leaf,
Nature's own jest, a world full of grieve.

The breeze chuckles loud, in a playful jest,
As blossoms break out in a flowery fest.
With whispers of pollen, they tease the bees,
A sneaky romance in the swaying trees.

Sweetly Woven

A tapestry spun with colors so bright,
Insects parade, oh what a sight!
Petals giggle, brook chuckles too,
Nature's own farce, for me and for you.

Here comes a squirrel, with acorn in hand,
His dance in the grass, quite unplanned!
He slips on the petals, his pride makes a fall,
And all of the flowers break into a sprawl.

Dancing Shadows on Green Grass

Shadows prance under the sun's warm embrace,
All flowers have gathered to join in the race.
A daffodil trips, falls flat on the ground,
But laughter erupts, it's joy that's profound.

Fairies are giggling, as gnomes take a bow,
The whole field's a stage, nature's vaudeville now.
A twist and a twirl, the daisies all squeal,
As they waltz with the wind in a whimsical reel.

Nectar-Laden Dreams in Flight

A ladybug wearing her polka-dot dress,
Flies high on the breeze, avoids the big mess.
While dragonflies buzz with an elegant wave,
In the field's grand party, they're the ones who rave.

The petals create a soft, blooming throne,
Where butterflies giggle and claim it their own.
They sip on the nectar, stealing the show,
While whispers of sweetness through the garden blow.

A Tinge of Rosy Magic

With a wink from the sun, a mischief begins,
The flowers conspire, oh where do we spin?
A rose rolls its eyes as a daisy tells jokes,
And the whole garden laughs, including the folks.

A puffy white cloud joins in on the fun,
Spilling raindrops like confetti, oh what a run!
All blooms take a bow as petals turn pink,
Nature's comedy, a wink and a blink.

Orchard's Canvas of Timeless Grace

In an orchard full of cheer,
Where fruit and laughter share,
A squirrel stole my snack, oh dear!
With a cheeky little flair.

The trees dance with the breeze,
Buds giggle at the sun,
While bees hum their melodies,
As they buzz around for fun.

A rabbit hops on by,
Wearing shades like a star,
He winks with a sly eye,
As he munches on a carrot bar.

The colors bloom and play,
As bees throw a crazy bash,
In this funny, bright display,
Where even crows make a splash.

Budding Hopes of Early Days

A timid bud peeks out,
With a grin, it sways,
Saying, 'Check me out!'
As morning wakes and plays.

Little ants parade in line,
With tiny hats of clay,
They march with such design,
A wacky, leafy ballet.

A cloud floats by in glee,
And spills some drops of rain,
The flowers burst with spree,
Dancing in the joyful lane.

Each sprout has a joke to share,
With roots that tickle the ground,
In this garden of flair,
Laughter is always found.

Celestial Verses in Bloom

In the sky where colors twine,
Stars wink and have a laugh,
As moonlit petals intertwine,
In nature's quirky half.

Daisies wear their best tuxes,
Dress code: flowers at night,
With crickets serenading,
Under soft, silver light.

A comet zooms by with flair,
Stops to tease a blooming rose,
'You think you're the fairest there?'
'Oh please, just look at those!'

But petals giggle, play along,
As stardust sprinkles the ground,
In this cosmic, silly song,
Where joy is all around.

Nature's Canvas Awash in Pink

In a world brushed with pink,
Fairies paint with delight,
While dandelions wink,
It's a whimsical sight!

Butterflies in polka dots,
Tease the flowers in bloom,
While the toads in fancy spots,
Compose a froggy tune.

Breezes carry a jest,
As petals twirl and spin,
In a frolicsome quest,
Where do the giggles begin?

Every flower shares a grin,
With bumblebees in tow,
In this garden, fun's a win,
Where joyfulness will flow.

Petals in the Breeze

A flower sneezed, and petals flew,
The bees all laughed, as if they knew.
The sun shone bright, it winked with glee,
While ants held court beneath the tree.

A gust arrived, a swirling spree,
One blossom claimed it's chasing me!
A squirrel chuckled, what a sight,
As petals danced, all day and night.

Dandelions joined the crazy race,
As wildflowers made a funny face.
The big round moon began to giggle,
And twirled around, all wild and wiggle.

So if you see a furry bee,
Just wave hello, and let it be.
Nature plays the quirkiest pranks,
In fields of madness, laughter ranks.

Fragrant Promises

A sniff of scent, what's that I smell?
A fruit with plans, to cast a spell.
The apples crowed, in cheerful tones,
While pears played drums on acorn bones.

"Come join the feast!" a grape did shout,
While cherries bounced, and rolled about.
With every promise filled with glee,
A party brewed, just wait and see!

The citrus danced, a zesty jig,
And berries giggled, oh so big!
They made a toast, "To fruity fun!"
As laughter sparkled in the sun.

So grab your friends, don't miss the chance,
Where fragrant fruits lead the wild dance.
With every twist, a ripe delight,
You'll laugh and cheer with all your might.

Nature's Rosy Dance

In fields so wide, the colors swirl,
A rosy cheeked breeze began to twirl.
With each small bloom that joined the fun,
Nature grinned, for day was won.

A daisy waltzed with quite the flair,
While violets played, with vintage hair.
"Step to the left, then swing around!"
As daisies fell, no fear of ground.

The lilies blushed, in minty green,
They tossed their heads, like queens unseen.
The sun gave chase, a playful fiend,
In this grand ball, joy is convened.

With petals swirling, laughter burst,
Each bloom a step, each stem rehearsed.
In this ballet, wild and free,
Nature winks, "Come dance with me!"

Secrets Beneath the Orchard

In orchard depths, where secrets thrive,
The critters plot and giggle, alive.
A wily fox told tales so bold,
Of the juicy treasure, green and gold.

The rabbits gathered, ears all perked,
As whispers flew, and giggles lurked.
The groundhogs chimed in with a cheer,
"Let's dig and dance, the fruit is near!"

A squirrel dropped acorns, made a fuss,
"Don't tell the birds, it's just for us!"
The chipmunks snickered at their luck,
As fruits appeared, "Oh, what the pluck!"

So come and stroll, where laughter grows,
In shady nooks, where mischief flows.
The secrets here, nothing but fun,
In this orchard, where joy's begun.

When Petals Fall Like Dreams

When petals tumble down with grace,
I laugh as they land on my face.
A gentle breeze begins to play,
Making all my troubles sway.

Silly bees buzz all around,
In each flower, laughter's found.
They dance and swirl in the air,
As if they've forgotten their care.

The sun above has a mischievous grin,
While I dance, losing to win.
Each petal whispers a cheeky joke,
And even grumpy clouds provoke.

So here I stand, in nature's blend,
With petals, laughter, and a friend.
Springtime's mischief plays its tricks,
In this garden of giggles and flicks.

A Tapestry of Fragrance

In a garden where scents collide,
I trip on petals, feeling pride.
Each whiff a silly little tease,
Making me sneeze like a sneezy breeze.

Colors clash in a riot of cheer,
Red and yellow, oh so near.
A bluebird cackles on the fence,
Telling jokes that make no sense.

The flowers wink, they know the game,
As butterflies circle, saying my name.
I can't help but twirl around,
In this fragrant circus, joy is found.

So let's raise a glass to blooms galore,
With giggles and laughter, who could ask for more?
For spring's a party, come join the fun,
Where even the sun can't help but run!

Spring's Gentle Lullaby

Oh, the beauty in morning light,
When flowers start their giggling fight.
The daffodils wear a silly hat,
While busy ants plan just where to chat.

A breeze whispers soft lullabies,
As birds chirp jokes, oh what a surprise!
Leaves twirl down, caught in the flow,
Like a dance-off, ready to show.

Mice play tag beneath the trees,
While squirrels chase, as quick as bees.
Sounds of spring, a joyful song,
In nature's choir, we all belong.

So let's frolic in the sun,
With laughter and love, let's have our fun.
For every bloom sings a tune,
That tickles our hearts, morning to noon.

Hues of Hope

In the garden of colors bright,
A rainbow sprinkles pure delight.
Each petal shines with playful flair,
As I tumble down without a care.

The violet giggles, the pinks high-five,
This party's booming, feel them thrive!
With every scent, a joke unfolds,
Nature's humor never gets old.

Rabbits hop in their colorful boots,
Sharing laughs, while nibbling roots.
Underneath bluebell boon,
We dance with shadows to a cheerful tune.

So gather round, let joy expand,
In this garden, hand in hand.
Where hues of laughter paint the day,
In colors of hope that forever stay.

Time in Petals

In a garden where everyone sings,
A flower danced and lost its rings.
Bees in tuxedos buzzing around,
Claiming the best pollen this town found.

There's a ladybug giving a cheer,
With a top hat and a pint of beer.
They twirl and stomp on soft, green grass,
Making all the petals giggle and sass.

A snail got stuck in a slow-motion race,
While butterflies certainly picked up the pace.
With a 'pop' and a 'splat' they burst like a joke,
Flowers laughed till they nearly choked.

Time moves silly in this lovely spot,
Where even the sun seems to dance a lot.
So raise a glass to petals in bloom,
Where laughter is found in every room.

Nature's Joyful Parade

A squirrel wears shades, strutting in style,
On a nutty float, he goes a great mile.
With acorns galore, he twirls with delight,
Shouting, 'Catch me if you can!' in pure flight.

The birds chirped tunes like a band on a spree,
With tunes made of laughs and a touch of glee.
Hopping and flapping, they sang oh-so-loud,
As flowers rejoiced, well, they were quite proud.

A playful centipede leads a grand line,
While worms tumble down, oh how they entwine!
The daisies giggle, 'Look at them go!'
In this parade, there's no room for woe.

Laughs echo bright in this vibrant display,
Where nature throws parties on a sunny day.
With petals aplenty, joy fills the air,
In this whimsical world, there's fun everywhere.

Exquisite Encounters

Oh, what happened to that blooming rose?
It tried to whistle but sneezed and froze!
With a puff and a flurry, it covered its face,
While daisies were rolling, getting into the chase.

A bumblebee buzzed with a plan most grand,
To join a disco—was it really unplanned?
Dipped in nectar, it spun and did twirl,
While tulips clapped, looking all a-swirled.

The lilacs held hands, doing a jig,
As daffodils wiggled, it wasn't quite big.
They laughed with such flair, their petals aflame,
Turning this garden into a wild game.

In this riot of color, joy springs about,
With every encounter, there's laughter, no doubt.
So join in the fun, let the petals beam,
As nature's delight forms a whimsical dream.

An Overture of Blossoms

Once a tree thought it could sing a tune,
But strummed its branches, and down fell the moon!
With apples all rolling, a slippery show,
A chorus of chuckles, they all fell below.

The wind threw a party, with gusts full of cheer,
It belly-laughed loud as it whistled near.
Leaves fluttered up in a game of charades,
While flowers exchanged their bright masquerades.

A mouse wore a flower, looking quite swell,
Telling everyone tales, like a jolly old spell.
As petals all giggled and swayed with the breeze,
The spectacle grew, bringing laughs with such ease.

So dance with the breezes, lose track of your cares,
For every few minutes, there's joy in the airs.
This overture of laughter, in sun's gentle glow,
Builds harmony sweet, as blossoms bestow.

Silence Among the Petals

In the garden, whispers fly,
As bees buzz and butterflies sigh.
Petals giggle, soft and bright,
Tickling grass in the warm sunlight.

A snail slips on a slicky flower,
Claiming it's a very fine tower.
Ants march in a goofy parade,
While the daisies chuckle, unafraid.

Bees wear shades while sipping nectar,
Dancing like they're a hip contractor.
In this world, all is absurd,
Where even branches bend and curd.

Laughter blooms in every hue,
As mismatched blooms share their view.
What a sight, this floral spree,
In the giggly garden of glee!

A Tangle of Dreams

Once upon a twinkle bright,
A bumblebee had quite a fright.
Swirling thoughts on petals soft,
As daydreams take a silly loft.

A feathered friend sings a tune,
While chasing shadows beneath the moon.
The daisies shake in pure delight,
Holding hands, they twist so tight.

A worm joins in with a wiggle dance,
Causing a flurry of petals to prance.
Then all the flowers laugh and sway,
In this zany, joyful ballet.

With every bloom, a story spun,
Of nature's joy, and wink, and fun.
In tangled dreams, we find our way,
In a whimsical world, come what may.

Rituals of the Earth

Underneath the arching trees,
A squirrel blushes in the breeze.
Mockingbirds draw faces in the sky,
As petals fall, oh my, oh my!

Toadstools gather for a feast,
With tiny chairs, they munch, at least.
Each bite is full of grassy cheer,
With mushrooms dancing, never fear.

Rabbits hop in their Sunday best,
Wearing hats for the wild west.
While roses roll their eyes in style,
This harvest brings a giggly smile.

In nature's play, all join the game,
With rustling leaves, and blooms so tame.
Celebrate this floral mirth,
In the silly whispers of the earth.

Petal-Drift Dreams

Floating gently on a breeze,
Petals wave with such great ease.
Wiggling worms host a sing-along,
As the night hums a funny song.

The nightingale wears a silly hat,
While the hedgehog tiptoes, oh so fat.
Stars peek in with a twinkling grin,
As moonlit laughter begins to spin.

Fairies tumble 'neath the bloom,
Creating light in the darkened room.
A jolly jig in the summer night,
With petals drifting, oh, what a sight!

In this realm of petals so bright,
Where dreams take off like a kite.
Here's to the joy that nature brings,
In whimsical wonders, funny things.

Love Letters of Petals

In a garden where petals sway,
Love notes drift in a comical way.
Each bloom pens a letter so bright,
Signing off with a giggle and light.

Bees read them with buzzing delight,
While ants march in, what a silly sight!
With ink made of dew, it drips a bit,
A letter from roses, but they never quit!

Clovers exchange tales of their bloom,
Laughing at dandelions' fuzzy costume.
A peony blushes, 'Oh, what a tease!'
As petals throw confetti in the breeze.

So next time you stroll through fields so grand,
Hear the whispers of flowers, hand in hand.
For love may be fleeting, but laughter will stay,
In the garden where silly blooms play.

Through the Apples' Eyes

In a tree where apples giggle and gloat,
They watch as the wind makes a funny note.
With cheeks swelled red, they whisper and laugh,
About the poor pear who fell in the path.

One said, 'Look how that leaf danced away!'
'That's no leaf,' cried the other, 'it's here to stay!'
The birds join in with a flappy cheer,
As the apples share secrets that tickle the ear.

A caterpillar crawls, wearing a grin,
'This garden's my stage, let the fun begin!'
They cheer him on, 'You're the best of the bunch!'
As he wobbles and tumbles, oh what a hunch!

Through the branches they plot for a grand show,
A dance-off between the fruit is in flow.
So if you see apples with sparkles so sly,
Know they're up to mischief beneath the bright sky!

A Petal's Journey

Once a petal set sail on a breeze,
Hoping to travel, do anything to please.
With hopes held high, it flew past the road,
But got tangled in hair—oh, what a load!

A lady laughed loud, 'You dance like a fool!'
As the petal hung on, what a wobbly tool!
Soon it was freed, in a whirl and a twirl,
Off to the next adventure to unfurl.

It spotted a pond with a leaping frog,
Who croaked out a joke, 'You're a flashy smog!'
They chuckled together as the sun dipped low,
Who knew a petal could be quite the show?

When night descended, it nested quite snug,
In a patch of daisies, feeling the plug.
So remember, dear friends, as you stroll on by,
Every petal's a laugh, floating up to the sky!

Garden of Delicate Dreams

In a realm where giggles bloom bright and bold,
Petals whisper secrets, their stories retold.
A snapdragon nods, 'What a comical scene!'
While daisies wear sunglasses, all prim and pristine.

Sunflowers are gossiping, heads bowed low,
About the violets' dance at last night's show.
They twirled and they swayed, were quite the delight,
Until one tripped over—a real flower fright!

Bumblebees buzzed in, with a wink and a grin,
'Join us for nectar, we'll make quite a din!'
But one little bee flew straight for a hat,
And landed on a snail—oh, imagine that!

As twilight arrived, the moon took its cue,
In this garden of dreams, where laughter grew.
So tiptoe through petals, with joy in your heart,
For this whimsical place is a true work of art!

A Symphony of Pink

In gardens bright with hues divine,
The little bugs hold hands in line.
They dance around, a silly crew,
While thinking they have much to do.

A chicken peeks from yonder bush,
Claiming she can dance, then rush!
She takes a step, then slips away,
Yet laughs and says, "It's just ballet!"

A breezy tune floats through the air,
While all the birds start to declare:
"Who needs a throne when skies are clear?
We're the true jesters, far and near!"

So bring the smiles, the joy, the fun,
In fields of laughter, everyone!
A symphony of pink, you see,
Where nature sings in harmony!

Blooming in Sunshine

A dandelion wore a crown,
And shouted, "Look at me, I'm brown!"
While daisies giggled near the fence,
Said, "That's not fair, but we're not dense!"

A squirrel in shades strutted by,
He said, "I'm off to catch a fly!"
With every jump and every twist,
He fluffed his tail and couldn't resist.

"Hey Mr. Sun, don't shine so bright,
You're making all the bees take flight!"
But soon they buzzed and swarmed around,
In sweet chaos, they became renowned.

In laughter's grip, the flowers sway,
As sunshine paints the perfect day.
With every bloom and cheeky grin,
The world feels light; let joy begin!

Tender Blooms and Bright Skies

A butterfly wore polka dots,
And twirled through gardens, lots of slots.
"Look at me dance!" it chortled loud,
While tulips begged, "Please form a crowd!"

Through patches green, a rabbit hops,
Falls in a pile where daisies plop.
"Excuse me, flowers, I need some space,
Your pretty stems are taking place!"

A wind gust came, and hats took flight,
Amidst the blooms, it was pure delight.
They laughed and chased, a playful show,
Tender blooms in a vibrant row!

The sun looks down with cheerful rays,
As nature sings in funny ways.
Embrace the joy; let worries cease,
In a world where every bloom's a tease!

Chasing the Sun's Embrace

The ladybugs threw a sunlit ball,
It bounced away, they gave a call.
"Hey, come back here, you tricky sprite,
You know this game, it's pure delight!"

A sneaky ant wore tiny shades,
Claimed all his friends were like parades.
With marching steps, they tromp along,
Singing silly tales, a funny song.

The cloud put on a fluffy wig,
While grasshoppers hopped with a gig.
And in their dance beneath the sky,
They made a plan to reach up high!

With every bloom that brightens views,
The world feels light, like vibrant hues.
Chasing the sun and all its cheer,
Nature's playground, drawing us near!

Bees and Blossoms Ballet

In a garden, the bees took flight,
Dancing flowers under sunlight.
Buzzing here, then buzzing there,
Wings a-flutter, without a care.

Pollen suits and tiny shoes,
Wobbling round like they're on cruise.
Flirty petals doing a jig,
Who knew blooms could also gig?

Hives are rocking to nature's beat,
While lazy ants shuffle their feet.
With every sip from nectar's cup,
Honey dreams swirl and bubble up.

Laughter blooms where colors collide,
In a floral frolic, we abide!
Nature's chorus, a riot of fun,
Who knew gardening's work could run?

A Tidal Wave of Color

A splash of pink upon the ground,
Like candy clouds with petals round.
Splash! A yellow here or there,
Turning heads with burst of flair.

Nature's palette spills and flows,
A painter's dream, as wild wind blows.
Sassy greens and purples winks,
Bold designs in floral drinks!

Squirrels stop, then blink then giggle,
As rainbows dance, their tails a wiggle.
Nature's humor, endlessly bright,
A colorful circus, pure delight!

From seeds to blooms, a vibrant ride,
Joy emerges like the spring tide.
When blooms burst forth, oh what a sight,
Laughter blossoms from morn 'til night!

Frames of Floral Whimsy

In frames of green, a silly show,
Petals posing, stealing the glow.
Daffodils wear hats made of dew,
And roses giggle in shades of blue.

A daisy winks, a tulip bows,
As butterflies inquire, "Who's that clown?"
Funky stems in funky shoes,
In this floral game, everyone grooves!

Petals dance like they're on air,
Snapping selfies without a care.
Snap! Snap! the blossoms cheer,
In this wild gallery, smiles appear.

Each bloom a character, bright and bold,
Capturing moments, stories told.
As quirkiness fills the fragrant space,
In frames of whimsy, we find our place!

Journeys of the Heart

Oh, the adventures blooms can seek,
Wandering wide, with a playful sneak.
Petal-packed bags, they're ready to roam,
In a world of color, they find their home.

Through fields of giggles, they sway with ease,
Tales of pollen whispered by the breeze.
Every stop is a chance to play,
As they frolic in sunshine's ray!

Sticky sweet with honey thoughts,
Wondrous beings, in laughter caught.
A journey filled with joy and cheer,
With whispers of spring to endear.

In every heart, a seed is sown,
And like flowers, we've brightly grown.
So, dance and laugh as colors chart,
The whimsical journey of the heart!

The Unfolding of Color

A bud sat up, said "Hey there!"
With colors bright, danced in the air.
Winks from petals, a flower parade,
Stirred the bees to come invade.

Bees wore goggles, ready to munch,
Buzzing loudly, they'd have a crunch.
Sticky fingers, they steal the show,
Sipping nectar, putting on a glow.

The sun chuckled, showing his face,
While flowers twirled in nature's space.
Pollination, a clumsy affair,
With pollen stuck in every hair.

Colors collide in this wild scene,
Smiles and laughter, oh what a dream!
Each bloom giggles, a humorous sight,
As nature unfolds, pure, colorful light.

Makers of Sweetness

In a garden of glee, where joy takes flight,
The critters gather, a whimsical sight.
With tiny aprons and chef hats too,
They mix up flavors, all fresh and new.

One squirrel claimed to be the best chef,
While juggling acorns, he nearly fell!
A raccoon chimed in, flipped pancakes high,
Couldn't catch them—now they're stuck in the sky!

A ladybug danced on a cupcake top,
While ants formed lines at the candy shop.
"Gimme that sugar!" the bumblebees cried,
As the garden giggled, sweetness amplified.

Spoons in the air, they all took a bite,
Delightful chaos under moonlight.
The laughter swirled in sweet harmony,
Creating treats for all to see!

Emblems of Renewal

A hedgehog snoozed, snuggled tight so warm,
Woke in spring, to the cutest charm.
With a yawn and stretch, it tumbled about,
Spreading new vibes, no room for doubt.

Baby rabbits bounced, so spry and quick,
Leaping in circles, they'd do a trick.
With floppy ears flying up and down,
They'd practice their dance across the town.

Worms from below, put on a show,
Forming conga lines, all in a row.
Grinning and grooving in rich, dark soil,
Making the earth healthy with all their toil.

The trees, they chuckle, as blossoms burst,
Casting confetti; spring comes first!
With each new bloom, the laughter grows,
As nature shows off in delightful throws.

Threads of Nature's Fabric

A spider spins with elegance rare,
Creating tapestries that dance through air.
The wind giggles, as it gives a twirl,
Pulling threads tight, causing colors to swirl.

A butterfly slipped, fell in a patch,
Landed in mud, couldn't find a match.
"Where's my glam?" she exclaimed with glee,
As the ladybugs rolled, all wild and free.

Crickets chirped in a rhythmic beat,
In their own band, they rocked the street.
While fireflies flashed like disco lights,
Lighting up the night, oh what delights!

Nature's loom weaves laughter in steps,
With flowers prancing and gnomes in creps.
Each vibrant thread, a joyful trace,
Creating smiles in this magical place.

The Blooming Promise of Tomorrow

In springtime's grasp, a bud unfurls,
It's like a secret between the squirrels.
With petals dressed in swirls of pink,
They giggle softly, I think, I think!

In gardens where the sunlight beams,
They toss about like playful dreams.
A dance of blossoms, a whimsical show,
Who knew flowers could steal the show?

Bees wearing hats, quite dapper and neat,
Buzzing and swirling, a comic repeat.
While blooms are plotting their next grand feat,
Winning the title of Nature's sweet treat!

So here's to the buds and their blooming fun,
They paint the world when spring has begun.
With laughter wrapped in color's delight,
They promise joy from morning to night.

Kaleidoscope of Serene Moments

Petals parade, oh what a sight,
A swirling chaos in soft sunlight.
Dresses of colors, zealous and bright,
Nature's jesters in joyful flight.

Bees in tuxedos, new styles to flaunt,
Whispering secrets, a sweet little taunt.
They jiggle, they buzz, with something to share,
In blooms' sweet laughter, delight is laid bare.

Chasing each petal, the butterflies prance,
Twisting and twirling, a floral dance.
Though bees mockingly point, what a fun little game,
Nature's humor, too bright to be tame!

Buds make a promise behind leafy screens,
To burst into giggles, whatever that means!
In this garden canvas, amid giggles and cheer,
Every moment's a keeper, oh dear, oh dear!

Voices of the Fruitful Grove

In the grove where laughter awakes,
Fruitful voices share silly fakes.
An apple whispered to a cheeky pear,
"Watch out for gravity, it's just not fair!"

A ripe orange rolled, with a playful grin,
Challenging apples, they can't tumble in.
Beneath branches tangled in giggly vines,
Nature's jesters spin delightful lines.

A curious bird swooped in with flair,
Singing of sweetness beyond compare.
But each fruit winked, with secrets to hold,
A treasure trove of laughter, bright and bold!

So when you wander through this merry spot,
Recall the tales of the fruit that laughed a lot.
For humor exists in the green, lush throng,
Where each joke blossoms, and sings its song.

Silent Beauty in the Orchard

In twilight hush, the flowers giggle,
Whispers of petals, a quiet wiggle.
This ornate chandelier of funky blooms,
Shapes peculiar, like jester costumes.

Gentle breezes play hide and seek,
With each soft laugh, the blossoms peek.
Combining colors in clumsy arrays,
They chuckle softly through the day.

Behind each leaf lies a grinning secret,
Each flower plotting the next great feat.
In silent beauty, their humor grows,
Even the starlight knows how it goes.

So tread lightly in this orchard of glee,
Where laughter and elegance roam wild and free.
In stillness, there's joy like a springtime fling,
Where even silence begins to sing!

Petal-Laced Memories Whispered

In the garden, a dance takes flight,
Petals twirl in blissful delight.
A squirrel attempts a grand pirouette,
Tumbles and rolls, but no need to fret.

Bumblebees giggle, buzzing in glee,
While tulips whisper, 'Come join me!'
A butterfly slips on a dew-kissed petal,
Hilarity ensues in this wild metal.

The wind joins the laughter, a cheeky breeze,
Rustling the leaves, shaking the trees.
Nature's comedy, full of surprise,
Let's toss confetti as laughter rises!

In this arena of colors, we play,
Chasing our worries and woes away.
With every bloom, a chuckle's released,
In this party of petals, we dance and feast.

The Unfolding Story of Spring

Spring rolls in, like a jolly old friend,
With stories of joy that never shall end.
A tulip snickers, its color too bright,
While daffodils' hats take up quite a sight.

Old trees crack jokes with a creaky sound,
As rabbits hop by, all merry and round.
A gopher pops up with a giggling grin,
Whispering tales of the mischief within.

The sky's a canvas, splashed with pure cheer,
Clouds play hide and seek, drawing near.
One cloud jokes, "I'm off to make rain!"
While others laugh, "Just don't cause a train!"

Spring's unfolding chapters are penned with delight,
Laughter and blossoms shine poems in light.
With each new bloom, a giggle does swell,
In the heart of the season, all's merry and well.

Beneath a Canopy of Pink

Underneath the cotton-candy skies,
Petals fall gently, a sweet surprise.
A dog prances by, slipping on a spree,
Slightly embarrassed, he shakes with glee.

Children laugh, chasing butterflies,
While a flower throws shade, making sly sighs.
A robin drops down, hops over to tease,
Singing a tune that'll tickle the trees.

With every bloom, feels like a big hug,
The ground's a soft blanket, so warm and snug.
Squirrels play tag and the breeze flirts with leaves,
In this playful arena, the heart never grieves.

Beneath this pink heaven, we gather and smile,
For moments like these are worth every mile.
A comedy show where the nature's the star,
Beneath this grand canopy, we feel who we are.

Laughter of Bees and Blossoms

Buzzing bees crack jokes as they zoom about,
Pollen parties, and they never pout.
A blossom giggles as it sways in the breeze,
"Hey little bee, can you give me a tease?"

A buzzing brigade in a floral parade,
"I'll pollinate you!" the bold bee relayed.
While daisies chuckle, sharing sweet dreams,
Of sunshine and rain and the sweetest of schemes.

A dandelion grins, "I'll make a wish!"
While petunias tease him, "Not quite delish!"
With every pitter-patter, laughter's released,
Among rows of petals, the joy's never ceased.

In this garden of giggles, mischief's the name,
With bees as our jesters, there's never a shame.
So join in the fun, come dance on the green,
For laughter's the nectar in this whimsical scene.

www.ingramcontent.com/pod-product-compliance
Lightning Source LLC
Chambersburg PA
CBHW062107280426
43661CB00086B/285